The Tao
and
the Bard

Also by Phillip DePoy

The Tao
and
the Bard

A Conversation

Moderated by
Phillip DePoy

ARCADE PUBLISHING · NEW YORK

Copyright © 2013 by Phillip DePoy

All Rights Reserved. No part of this book may be reproduced in any manner without the express written consent of the publisher, except in the case of brief excerpts in critical reviews or articles. All inquiries should be addressed to Arcade Publishing, 307 West 36th Street, 11th Floor, New York, NY 10018.

Arcade Publishing books may be purchased in bulk at special discounts for sales promotion, corporate gifts, fund-raising, or educational purposes. Special editions can also be created to specifications. For details, contact the Special Sales Department, Arcade Publishing, 307 West 36th Street, 11th Floor, New York, NY 10018 or arcade@skyhorsepublishing.com.

Arcade Publishing® is a registered trademark of Skyhorse Publishing, Inc.®, a Delaware corporation.

Visit our website at www.arcadepub.com.

Visit the author's website at www.phillipdepoy.com

10 9 8 7 6 5 4 3 2 1

Library of Congress Cataloging-in-Publication Data is available on file.

ISBN: 978-1-61145-838-1

Printed in the United States of America

Introduction

Shakespeare and Lao Tzu have a good deal in common.

Lao Tzu was the Great Archivist during the Zhou dynasty of China in the sixth century BCE. When he left the archives to retire into the mountains, a city guard, recognizing great wisdom, prevented Lao Tzu from leaving until the old man wrote down everything he had learned, everything that was important to know. The archivist paused long enough to compose the *Tao Te Ching*, and then vanished.

Lao Tzu's work is generally arranged as eighty-one short verses, and its title is sometimes translated to mean *The Book of the Way of Virtue*. (*Tao* means "road" or "path" but also "the way of nature," or "the road of ultimate reality." *Te* means "virtue," "character," "moral force" or "power." *Ching* means "book.")

By the middle of the twentieth century most scholars began insisting that the *Tao Te Ching* would have to be the product of many writers, written from a vast array of source materials over the course of centuries, and that Lao Tzu, as a historical figure, did not exist at all.

Some scholars believe that Shakespeare did not write Shakespeare, or did not exist at all, at least not as a singular poet of the English language. At the very least, it is suggested that the author stole wholeheartedly from his contemporaries. Certainly not a single one of Shakespeare's plots is original to the author. All thirty-eight works are based on ideas, characters, even snips of dialogue from works of literature or theatre that predate Shakespeare, sometimes by a thousand years. Some believe that *Hamlet*, 1600–01, for example, was taken almost entirely from Thomas Kyd's 1589 play of the same name, down to the "To be or not to be" speech. Shakespeare's first play, *Henry VI, Part 1* (1589–90) was taken, in great part, from Hall's *The Union of the Two Noble and Illustrious Families of Lancaster and York* (1548) and Holinshed's *Chronicles* (1587). Arguably, his last play, *The Tempest* (1611), used everything from Jourdain's *Discovery of the Bermudas* to Ovid's *Metamorphoses* for inspiration. Each one of his plays, in fact, owes a debt to similar source material.

Ultimately, of course, that kind of criticism doesn't matter. Every playwright of his day did the same thing; and a hundred playwrights who look at the same facts will produce a hundred different plays. The beauty of the work lies less in the source material than in the language. But scholars still debate Shakespeare's abilities, even his existence, some insisting that his work is the product of many authors put forth under the single, invented character of "Shakespeare."

The Tao and the Bard is a simple conversation between these two phantasms, in their own words, arranged in the traditional order according to Lao Tzu's eighty-one verses. The exact purpose or meaning of this conversation is as elusive as the perfect interpretation of any of Shakespeare's great soliloquies, and as impossible to explain as any verse in the *Tao*. (It should be noted that the traditional eighty-one verses of the *Tao Te Ching* are longer and more complex than the excerpts used for this book.)

Still, something is illuminated by any conversation between Western creative ideas and Eastern mysticism. Joseph Campbell, Alan Watts, D. T. Suzuki, Jiddu Krishnamurti, Christmas Humphries, Ursula Le Guin, Fritjof Capra—thousands of people, in fact, have worked to bridge the gap between Eastern and Western thought, for the purpose of a greater understanding and mutual enlightenment.

The hope is that the conversation in this book might provide a diverting footnote to that larger effort.

A Word about Spelling

Further complicating the question of identity for both of these historical figures is the spelling of their names. Both writers have suffered, over the centuries, from the tyranny of scholars who disagree with the often quoted dictum: "It is a damn poor mind that can think of only one way to spell a word." (A sentiment variously attributed to Thomas Jefferson, Andrew Jackson, and Mark Twain.)

Of course, in the case of Lao Tzu the issue is mainly one of transliteration, trying to make Roman letters create a word that will sound the way a Chinese pictogram (老子) is pronounced. So his name has been given, at various times, as Laozi, Lǎozǐ, Lao Tzu, Laotse, Lao Tu, Lao-Tsu, Laotze, Laosi, Laocius and, in all probability, a hundred other iterations. I personally prefer Lao Tzu because it's a name comprised of two words (for the sake of yin and yang, the Tao's guiding principle) and each word is three letters (for the sake of Lao Tzu's suggestion that "From three all things come" in verse forty-two of the *Tao*).

In Shakespeare's world, this complication is, at least in part, the playwright's own fault. Of the six signatures known to exist that were written by Shakespeare himself, each has a different spelling: Willm Shakp. William Shaksper, Wm Shakspe, William Shakspere, Willm Shakspere, and, finally, "By me William Shakspeare." All of these signatures appear on legal documents (court papers, a mortgage, his will). And none of these spellings is the one in current preferred usage. In this particular instance, I prefer to agree with the playwright when he says, "What's in a name? That which we call a rose, by any other name would smell as sweet."

No matter how it's spelled.

The Tao
and
the Bard

One

LAO TZU:

> The Tao that can be said in words is not the Tao.
> Words cannot describe it.

SHAKESPEARE:

> Words, words, mere words, no matter from the
> heart.
>> Troilus, *Troilus and Cressida*, act V, scene iii

> Polonius: What do you read, my lord?
> Hamlet: Words, words, words.
>> *Hamlet*, act II, scene ii

> Words are but wind.
>> Dromio, *The Comedy of Errors*, act III, scene i

COMMENT: The word *sun* doesn't give any warmth or light. Only the sun can do that. Saying the word is only meant to suggest the thing itself. Of course, in the case of Lao Tzu or Shakespeare, the irony of using words to say something that can't be said in words is significant. Lao Tzu's writing is a foundation of Eastern thought. Shakespeare's plays are among the greatest uses of any Western language.

Two

LAO TZU:

> In each perception of good,
> there are the seeds of evil.

SHAKESPEARE:

> There is some soul of goodness in things evil.
> Henry, Henry V, act IV, scene i

LAO TZU:

> What is true and what is not true exist together.
> Great and small are complementary,
> before and after make sequence,
> long and short are relative.

SHAKESPEARE:

> The bold and coward,
> The wise and fool, the artist and unread,
> The hard and soft, all seem affined [affiliated] and
>   kin.
> Troilus and Cressida, act I, scene iii

COMMENT: The world is defined by opposites. Every ancient spiritual text begins with the separation of light from darkness, water from land, man from woman. Lao Tzu seems to insist that opposites create each other: once anything is described as *right*, that necessarily implies something else that's *wrong*. As for Shakespeare, his greatest characters all contain elements of both good and evil: Othello is filled with love and rage; Hamlet suffers cowardice and bravery; Macbeth knows murder and remorse. That's what makes them true.

Three

Lao Tzu:

> Be silent while you work
> and keep control over all.

Shakespeare:

> I like your silence, it the more shows off your
> wonder.
>> Paulina, *The Winter's Tale*, act V, scene iii

Comment: If words aren't the way to tell the truth, silence ought to have its say.

Four

LAO TZU:

Tao is the elemental nothing
from which all things are born,
a deep pool into which all things go.

SHAKESPEARE:

The elements of whom your swords are temper'd
    may as well
Wound the loud winds, or with
bemock'd-at-stabs
Kill the still-closing waters.

Ariel, *The Tempest*, act III, scene iii

LAO TZU:

It blunts sharpness and levels mountains.
An eternal void, it is eternally filled.

SHAKESPEARE:

O God! that one might read the book of fate,
Make mountains level, and the continent
Melt itself into the sea! And changes fill the cup
    of alteration.

Henry, *Henry IV, Part 2*, act III, scene i

LAO TZU:

When you lose yourself, you will be everywhere.

SHAKESPEARE:

I have lost myself, I am not here.
Romeo, *Romeo and Juliet*, act I, scene i

———

COMMENT: "Elemental nothing" is the origin of all things. In the Hindu pantheon, it's the god who continually divides itself in half. In Taoism it manifests itself in nature. For Shakespeare, it's nature imbued with God. No matter how it's defined, it's where everything comes from and everything goes, and no force can prevail against it.

Five

LAO TZU:

> Is the world unkind?
> Nature burns up life like a straw dog.
> Should the wise man meet all things in nature
> and dismiss them as he would a straw dog?

SHAKESPEARE:

> Allow not nature more than nature needs,
> Man's life's as cheap as beast's.
> > Lear, *King Lear*, act II, scene iv

> She burnt with love, as straw with fire flameth;
> She burnt out love, as soon as straw outburneth
> > "The Passionate Pilgrim," poem 7

———

COMMENT: Nature has no emotion. A strong wind doesn't have malice when it tears apart a house. A fire isn't angry when it destroys a forest. A rose doesn't intend to be beautiful. Is there something to be learned from that?

Six

LAO TZU:

> The mystical feminine quality of the universe
> is eternal and ever present.
> It is the source of heaven and earth.
> Empty yet undiminished,
> it gives birth to the infinite.

SHAKESPEARE:

> From women's eye this doctrine I derive:
> They are the ground, the books, the academes,
> From whence doth spring true Promethean fire.
>> Berowne, *Love's Labor's Lost*, act IV, scene iii

COMMENT: In Sumerian religious texts, the oldest known records of religious philosophy on the planet, the first thing that existed was the primordial sea, also thought of as the goddess Nammu, the originator of all things.

Seven

LAO TZU:

> Because the world doesn't live for itself, it will
> live on;
> the unselfish are the only ones who find
> fulfillment.

SHAKESPEARE:

> For my single self, I had as lief not be
> as live to be in awe of such a thing as myself.
> > Cassius, *Julius Caesar*, act I, scene ii

COMMENT: Everyone agrees: don't be selfish. "For where you have envy and selfish ambition, there you find disorder and every evil practice" (James 3:16–17). "The common enemy of all religious disciplines is selfishness of mind" (The Dalai Lama). "All love is expansion, all selfishness is contraction" (Swami Vivekananda, on Hindu thought).

Eight

Lao Tzu:

> The highest good goes everywhere,
> nourishes all things without trying,
> both high and low, making the world One.

Shakespeare:

> The selfsame sun that shines upon his court
> hides not his visage from our cottage, but
> looks on alike.
>> Perdita, *The Winter's Tale*, act IV, scene iv

> All places that the eye of heaven visits
> are to a wise man ports and happy havens.
>> Gaunt, *Richard III*, act I, scene iii

———

COMMENT: If, as in verse five, nature doesn't have any personal responsibility for destroying a home, it follows that it also has no regard for wealth or power: the same sun warms a castle and a cottage, and everywhere it shines is sunny.

Nine

LAO TZU:

> To take all you want is never as good as to stop
> when you should.
> Wealth, power, lust, pride: all beget their own
> downfall.

SHAKESPEARE:

> Fie on lust and luxury,
> Lust is but a bloody fire
> Kindled with unchaste desire,
> Fed in heart whose flames aspire
> As thoughts do blow them higher and higher
> Pinch him and burn him and turn him about
> Till candles and starlight and moonshine be out.
>
> Fairies' Song to Falstaff,
> *The Merry Wives of Windsor*, act V, scene v

LAO TZU:

> Scheme and plot, and you won't keep riches long
> at all.
> As long as your house is full of gold and your
> pockets filled with money,
> it's all impossible to guard.

SHAKESPEARE:

See, sons, what things you are!
How quickly nature falls into revolt
When gold becomes her object.

Henry, *Henry IV, Part 2*, act IV, scene v

COMMENT: Everyone agrees. "It is easier for a camel to go through the eye of a needle than for a rich man to enter into the kingdom of God" (Matthew 19:24). "In no manner whatsoever do I declare that gold and silver be accepted or sought for" (The Buddha's Fire Sermon). "There is no hope of immortality through wealth" (The Brihadaranyaka Upanishad).

Ten

LAO TZU:

> Can you control the animal in your soul
> and still remain the same person always?
> Can you keep your mind from wandering
> and concentrate on one thing?
> This is the mystic virtue.

SHAKESPEARE:

> Keep yourself within yourself.
>> Charmian, *Antony and Cleopatra*, act II, scene iv

> I am constant as the northern star.
>> Caesar, *Julius Caesar*, act III, scene i

COMMENT: Great concentration—on a single thought, single activity, or single moment—is an essential quality for all human beings, and all too missing from contemporary life.

Eleven

LAO TZU:

> You can make a pot out of clay,
> but the useful part of the pot is not the clay,
> it's the part that's empty, where there is nothing.
> Nothingness is a great secret of the Tao.

SHAKESPEARE:

> The ear-deafening voice of the Oracle, kin to
>   Jove's thunder,
> so surprised my sense, that I was nothing.
>   Cleomenes, *The Winter's Tale*, act III, scene i

> Lear: Speak.
> Cordelia: Nothing, my lord.
> Lear: Nothing?
> Cordelia: Nothing.
>
>   *King Lear*, act I, scene i

COMMENT: A cup, no matter how beautiful or expensive it is, exists only to create an empty space into which something can be poured. The empty space is the important part. Maybe there's something to be learned from having empty places in ourselves. There's a great story about a student who explained to his teacher that he was eager to learn but already very advanced because he'd studied a lot at home. The teacher congratulated the student and offered him some tea. The student held out his cup and the teacher poured, but when the cup was filled, she kept on pouring. Finally the student said, "Excuse me, but you're spilling the tea, the cup is already full." The teacher said, "That's right. I can't teach you anything if you think your cup is already full. You have to bring me an empty cup."

Twelve

LAO TZU:

> The five colors blind your eyes,
> the five sounds will dull your ears,
> the five flavors mislead your taste;
> the wise follow the heart, not the senses.

SHAKESPEARE:

> In faith, I do not love thee with mine eye,
> For they in thee a thousand errors note,
> But 'tis my heart that loves what they despise,
> Who in despite of view is pleased to dote;
> Nor are mine ears with thy tongue's tune
>   delighted,
> Nor tender feelings to base touches prone,
> Nor taste, nor smell desire to be invited
> To any sensual feast with thee alone.
>
> Sonnet 141, lines 1–8

———

COMMENT: The senses can be completely illusory. It's easy to mistake a red autumn leaf for a cardinal flying to the ground. The Hebrew proverb says, "The heart sees better than the eyes."

Thirteen

LAO TZU:

It is said: "Good fortune and ill fortune cause
tension.
Creative and destructive natures exist equally in
the mind."
Tension exists because we have a mind,
and because that mind has dual purposes.
All things happen in the mind.

SHAKESPEARE:

There is nothing either good or bad, but thinking
makes it so.

Hamlet, *Hamlet*, act II, scene ii

All things are ready, if our minds be so.

Henry, *Henry V*, act IV, scene iii

LAO TZU:

Be free from thought.

SHAKESPEARE:

Thought is free.

Maria, *Twelfth Night*, act I, scene iii

COMMENT: There's a traditional story about two students looking at a flag flapping in the wind. One student says, "The wind is moving." The other student says, "No, the flag is moving." Their teacher says, "Both wrong, your mind is moving." That's only marginally more difficult to understand, at first, than this: why does one person smile and congratulate the other team when he loses a baseball game, while another person on the same losing team kicks things and curses? It's the same event, so maybe it has something to do with how the mind interprets the event. Taking this idea to its greatest extent, maybe everything depends on how the mind interprets it. And if that's the case, why wouldn't people choose to interpret everything happily?

Sixteen

LAO TZU:

> All things that come into existence
> return to the source,
> all things in nature
> return to the One.

SHAKESPEARE:

> As many arrows loosed several ways, come to
>   one mark,
> As many ways meet in one town,
> As many fresh streams meet in one salt sea . . .
> So may a thousand actions, once afoot, end in
>   one purpose.
>
> Canterbury, Henry V, act I, scene ii

COMMENT: A theory of the universe begins with the idea that in the beginning there was a void, and in the end everything will return to that void. In the Hindu pantheon that process happens over and over and over again in an endless succession of *kalpas*. Greek thinkers, especially Pythagoras, called this concept an Eternal Return: that the universe recurs an infinite number of times. Some contemporary scientists have posited a kind of "Big Crunch" at the ending of the "Big Bang," that eventually everything that exploded will come back together. Everything comes from some source, and will return to that source in the end.

Seventeen

Lao Tzu:

> If you have no faith in others,
> others will not trust you.
> When you have faith in others,
> others will do for themselves.

Shakespeare:

> Trust not him that hath once broken faith.
>> Elizabeth, *Henry VI, Part 3*, act IV, scene iv

> There's no more faith in thee than in a stewed
> prune.
>> Falstaff, *Henry IV, Part 1*, act III, scene iii

———

COMMENT: "Faith is taking the first step even when you don't see the whole staircase" (Martin Luther King, Jr.). "Faith is to believe what you do not see; the reward of this faith is to see what you believe" (Saint Augustine). "Faith is the bird that feels the light when the dawn is still dark" (Rabindranath Tagore). But also, of course, the opposite is also true: "Call on God, but row away from the rock." (Hunter S. Thompson).

Eighteen

Lao Tzu:

> When barren wisdom
> and intelligence appeared,
> great hypocrisy also came,
> and rules to govern our lives.

Shakespeare:

> And since the wisdom of their choice is rather
>   to have my hat than my heart,
> I will practice the insinuating nod and be off to
>   them most counterfeitly.
> Coriolanus, Coriolanus, act II, scene iii

COMMENT: When a certain kind of empty education is imposed on anyone, it's difficult to learn. This is especially true in educational institutions whose purpose is to teach rules, and adherence to those rules, instead of offering doorways to genuine knowledge.

Nineteen

LAO TZU:

Rid yourself of listening to philosophers!
Ignore all professors and those who depend on laws!

SHAKESPEARE:

Hang up philosophy!
Unless philosophy can make a Juliet,
Displant a town, reverse a prince's doom,
It helps not, it prevails not; talk no more.
Romeo, *Romeo and Juliet*, act III, scene iii

The first thing we do, let's kill all the lawyers!
Dick, *Henry VI, Part 2*, act IV, scene ii

LAO TZU:

Learn things yourself.
You'll profit a hundredfold.

SHAKESPEARE:

Learning is by an adjunct to ourself,
And where we are, our learning likewise is.
Berowne, *Love's Labor's Lost*, act IV, scene ii

Twenty

LAO TZU:

Without apparent direction I drift, seeming
homeless.
All others have plenty, I have none.
I am always confused.
Ordinary people sparkle, I am the only shadow.
Vulgar people seem happy, I alone am
melancholy.
I am lonely and different
because I live at the door to the All,
seeking entrance.

SHAKESPEARE:

I have neither the scholar's melancholy, which is
    emulation,
nor the musician's which is fantastical, nor the
    courtier's, which is proud,
nor the soldier's, which is ambitious, nor the
    lawyer's, which is politic,
nor the lady's, which is nice, nor the lover's,
    which is all these,
but it is a melancholy of mine own, compounded
    of many simples,

extracted from many objects, and indeed the
   sundry contemplation of my travels in which
   my often rumination wraps me in a most
   humorous sadness.
                              Jaques, *As You Like It*, act IV, scene i

O Melancholy,
Who ever yet could sound thy bottom? find . . .
Mightiest easiliest harbor in? Thou blessed
   thing,
Jove knows what man thou mightst have made,
   But I,
Thou diedst, a most rare boy, of melancholy.
                         Belarius, *Cymbeline*, act IV, scene ii

Armado: Boy, what sign is it that a man of great
   spirit grows Melancholy?
Moth: A great sign, sir, that he will look sad.
                         Love's Labor's Lost, act I, scene ii

———

COMMENT: One problem with following the path to
great knowledge is that it can sometimes be a unique,
individual path that separates you from everyone else.
You see things differently than anyone you know. You
can't be happy with your old life, the daily news, an
ordinary job. And sometimes, it has to be admitted,
that can be a little lonely or sad.

Twenty-one

LAO TZU:

Tao is like a dream,
invisible like the air.
In it there are images
elusive, evading,
essences that are difficult to discern
shadows cast by the real light.

SHAKESPEARE:

These our actors . . . were all spirits and are
   melted into air . . .
We are such stuff as dreams are made on.

> Prospero, *The Tempest*, act V, scene i

A dream itself is but a shadow.

> Hamlet, *Hamlet*, act II, scene ii

True, I talk of dreams
Which are the children of an idle brain.
Begot of nothing but vain fantasy,
Which is as thin of substance as the air
And more inconstant than the wind.

> Mercutio, *Romeo and Juliet*, act I, scene iv

Twenty-two

LAO TZU:

Tao makes crooked places straight,
rough places smooth,
fills the pools.
When there is no goal
everything succeeds.
It all comes to One in the end.

SHAKESPEARE:

All's one for that.
> Falstaff, *Henry IV*, *Part 1*, act II, scene iv

So they loved as love in twain
Had the essence but in one,
Two distincts, division none.
> "The Phoenix and Turtle," lines 25–27

COMMENT: It's impossible to deny the power of thinking that the universe is one single thing made up of everything.

Twenty-three

LAO TZU:

Nature is sparing in its speech,
so how much more should we all be.

SHAKESPEARE:

Brevity is the soul of wit.

Polonius, *Hamlet*, act I, scene v

COMMENT: Exactly.

Twenty-four

LAO TZU:

> Standing on tip-toe and overreaching,
> it's easy to fall.
> Doing too much will mean failure.

SHAKESPEARE:

> Who builds his hope in air of your good looks
> Lives like a drunken sailor on a mast,
> Ready with every nod to tumble down
> Into the fatal bowels of the deep.
>
> Hastings, Richard III, act III, scene iv

LAO TZU:

> And if you cling to your work,
> nothing you create will last.

SHAKESPEARE:

> Yesterday the word of Caesar might have stood
> against the world; now lies he there, and
> none so poor to do him reverence.
>
> Anthony, Julius Caesar, act III, scene ii

Small have continual plodders ever won
Save base authorities from others' books.

> Berowne, *Love's Labor's Lost*, act I, scene i

———

Comment: No matter how talented he is, no juggler can keep an infinite number of balls in the air; and, really, how many human beings are talented jugglers at all? Furthermore, most artists create great paintings for everyone to see, not to keep hidden away in a darkened studio.

Twenty-five

LAO TZU:

> The Tao is great,
> the sky is great,
> the earth is great,
> a soul is great.
> These four are great,
> and from these elements
> your soul is born,
> but your soul is only one of them.
> The soul follows the earth,
> the earth follows the sky,
> the sky follows the Tao,
> Tao follows its own nature.

SHAKESPEARE:

> Thou hast as chiding a nativity
> As fire, air, water, earth and heaven can make
> To herald thee from thy womb.
>
> Pericles, *Pericles*, act III, scene i

> The earth can have but earth, which is his due,
> My spirit is thine, the better part of me.
>
> Sonnet 74, lines 7–8

COMMENT: Each individual human spirit is significant and worthwhile, but it's not greater than the force that created it.

Twenty-six

LAO TZU:

A heavy stone is the foundation of a lighter house.
The truly wise are heavy and quiet at heart,
even in frivolous moods.

SHAKESPEARE:

Sad pause and deep regard beseem the sage.
The Rape of Lucrece, line 227

———

COMMENT: "Solitary trees, if they grow at all, grow strong" (Winston Churchill). "The word 'happiness' would lose its meaning if it were not balanced by sadness" (Carl Jung).

———

LAO TZU:

It is possible to travel all day
and not be separated from home.

SHAKESPEARE:

> A traveler! By my faith, you have great reason to be
> sad.
> You have sold your own lands to see other men's;
> then to
> have seen much, and to have nothing, is to have
> rich eyes.
> > Rosalind, *As You Like It*, act II, scene iv

> I, Costard, running out, that was safely within,
> Fell over the threshold and broke my shin.
> > Costard, *Love's Labor's Lost*, act III, scene i

———

COMMENT: This section of verse twenty-six of the *Tao* is too easy to interpret as meaning that imagination or reading or even, as some current scholars have suggested, universal media can take the place of physical traveling. Shakespeare seems to capture the loneliness and difficulty and even the reward of travel, but Lao Tzu's point seems to be more that all places are one place. (Wallace Stevens amplifies this notion in his poem "Metaphors of a Magnifico": "Twenty men crossing a bridge into a village are twenty men crossing twenty bridges into twenty villages, or one man crossing a single bridge into a village.")

Twenty-seven

LAO TZU:

A traveler who has no destination
will always arrive at the right place.

SHAKESPEARE:

And when I wander here and there, I then do
most go right.
Autolycus, *The Winter's Tale*, act IV, scene iii

LAO TZU:

The good ought to instruct the bad gently,
because the bad are the business of the good.
If the one does not love the instruction,
and the other love the business,
all things are out of sorts.

SHAKESPEARE:

The gentleman is learn'd and a most rare
speaker,
To nature none more bound; his training such
That he may furnish and instruct great teachers
And never seek for aid out of himself.
Henry, *Henry VII*, act I, scene ii

COMMENT: In Eugen Herrigel's book *Zen in the Art of Archery*, the author discovers, to his great surprise, that not caring about aiming at the target can produce a bull's-eye nearly every time. This is a practical application of Lao Tzu's first observation.

Twenty-eight

LAO TZU:

> Be aware of your masculine nature,
> but by keeping the feminine way. . .
> Be aware of the light all around you
> by knowing the darkness.
> Be aware of your honor and glory
> by receiving everything like water: endless and
> nothing.

SHAKESPEARE:

> My brain I'll prove the female to my soul,
> my soul the father, and these two beget a
>   generation.
> > Richard, *Richard II*, act V, scene v

> Where is any author in the world
> Teaches such beauty as a woman's eye?
> > Berowne, *Love's Labor's Lost*, act IV, scene iii

> Glory is like a circle in the water,
> Which never ceaseth to enlarge itself
> Till by broad spreading it disperse to nought.
> > Joan De Pucelle, *Henry VI, Part 1*, act I, scene ii

COMMENT: The concept of yin and yang is often represented by a circle that is half black and half white, divided by a curving, S-shaped line. Yin, the black half, is meant to be the universal feminine; Yang, the white half, is masculine. In the black half there is always a dot of white, in the white half there is always a dot of black. This is meant to indicate that there is always an element of one in the other. But, generally water is associated with the feminine power, and Tao seems to insist that nothing can prevail against water.

Twenty-nine

LAO TZU:

> Do not go to extremes,
> make sweeping judgments,
> or lead a life of excess.

SHAKESPEARE:

> They are as sick that surfeit with too much
> as they that starve with nothing.
> It is no mean happiness therefore to be seated in
>   the mean.
>
> > Nerissa, *The Merchant of Venice*, act I, scene ii

LAO TZU:

> When some are strong,
> others are weak,
> so the wise do not use their strength like tyrants.

SHAKESPEARE:

> It is excellent
> To have a giant's strength, but it is tyrannous
> To use it like a giant.
>
> > Isabella, *Measure for Measure*, act II, scene ii

COMMENT: This particular verse of the *Tao* is often said to be a political statement. Nations shouldn't be bullies. Shakespeare believed the same advice to be useful for monarchs.

———

LAO TZU:

Rid yourself of all extreme inclinations.

SHAKESPEARE:

Boundless intemperance
In nature is a tyranny; it hath been
The untimely emptying of the happy throne,
and fall of many kings.

Malcolm, *Macbeth*, act IV, scene iii

Thirty

LAO TZU:

Once you've made your point, don't brag.
Once you've won, don't gloat.
If you believe in yourself,
you won't need to convince others.
You'll behave toward others
as you treat yourself.

SHAKESPEARE:

Who knows himself a braggart, let him fear this;
for it will come to pass that every braggart shall
    be found an ass.

> Parolles, *All's Well That Ends Well*,
> act IV, scene iii

O never will I trust to speeches penned
Nor to the motion of a schoolboy's tongue,
Nor never come in visard to my friend,
Nor woo in rhyme like a blind harper's song!
Taffeta phrases, silken terms precise,
Three-piled hyperboles, spruce affection,
Figures pedantical—these summer flies
Have blown me full of maggot ostentation.

> Berowne, *Love's Labor's Lost*, act V, scene ii

Be to yourself as you would to your friend.

Norfolk, *Henry VIII*, act I, scene i

COMMENT: Once again, we all seem to agree. "That which you hate to be done to you, do not do to another" (from an ancient Egyptian papyrus, c. 664 BCE – 323 BCE). "Avoid doing what you would blame others for doing" (Thales, c. 624 BC – c. 546 BC). "Treat others as you treat yourself" (*Mahābhārata*). "As you would that men should do to you, do also to them likewise" (Jesus, in Luke 6:31).

Thirty-one

LAO TZU:

> Weapons should be avoided
> in favor or dignity.
> If weapons cannot be avoided,
> they must be used from the heart,
> with restraint.

SHAKESPEARE:

> Now put your shields before your hearts,
> and fight with hearts more proof than shields.
> > Caius Martius, *Coriolanus*, act I, scene iv
>
> If he do fear God, he must necessarily keep peace;
> If he break the peace, he ought to enter into a
>   quarrel
> With fear and trembling.
> > Leontes, *Much Ado About Nothing*,
> > act II, scene iii

LAO TZU:

> War must always occasion Peace.

SHAKESPEARE:

> Make war breed peace.
> > Alcibiades, *Timon of Athens*, act V, scene iv

COMMENT: Verse thirty-two of the *Tao* is generally taken to be further political advice, this time about weapons and the use of war. "Men no longer debate whether armaments are a symptom or a cause of tension. The mere existence of modern weapons is a source of horror, and discord and distrust" (President John F. Kennedy).

Thirty-two

LAO TZU:

> The infinite has no name.
> Yet all things were born from
> and return to nature.
> And from nature all things
> draw virtues infinite.

SHAKESPEARE:

> Good alone is good, without a name.
> > King of France, *All's Well That Ends Well*,
> > > act II, scene iii

> What's in a name?
> > Juliet, *Romeo and Juliet*, act II, scene ii

> The earth that's nature's mother is her tomb,
> What is her burying grave, that is her womb;
> And from her womb children of divers kind
> We sucking on her natural bosom find:
> Many for many virtues excellent
> None but for some, and yet all different.
> > Friar Lawrence, *Romeo and Juliet*,
> > > act II, scene iii

COMMENT: In Genesis 2:19 we're told that "whatsoever Adam called every living creature, that *was* the name thereof." But the name of a thing doesn't capture the essence of that thing. The word *rose* doesn't smell at all, and even if a rose were called a *hammer* it would still have a sweet scent. Better to look at the essences of things and people, instead of their names.

Thirty-three

Lao Tzu:

> It is wisdom to know others,
> it is enlightenment to know one's self.

Shakespeare:

> This above all, to thine own self be true
> And it must follow as the night the day
> Thou canst not then be false to any man.
> > Polonius, *Hamlet*, act I, scene iii

> I know myself now, and I feel within me
> A peace above all earthly dignities,
> A still and quiet conscience.
> > Wolsey, *Henry VIII*, act III, scene ii

COMMENT: According to the Greek writer Pausanias, the aphorism "Know Thyself" was inscribed into the Temple of Apollo at Delphi. Further Greek commentary on that phrase adds that it especially applies to anyone whose "boasts exceed what they are." It also is meant to encourage everyone to give very little attention to popular or majority opinion.

Thirty-four

LAO TZU:

> Tao is everywhere and everything,
> but it is modest—it seems poor and small.
> Because of this, it cannot be false,
> it shines with great truth.

SHAKESPEARE:

> Falseness cannot come from thee,
> For thou lookest modest as Justice,
> And thou seemest a palace
> For the crown'd Truth to dwell in.
> > Pericles, *Pericles*, act V, scene i

Thirty-five

LAO TZU:

> Knowing the Form without form,
> you can go everywhere and fear no evil.

SHAKESPEARE:

> All form is formless, order orderless . . .
> Thou mayst hold a serpent by the tongue,
> A cased lion by the mortal paw,
> A fasting tiger safer by the tooth.
> > Pandulph, *The Life and Death of King John*,
> > > act II, scene i

> O place, O form,
> How often dost thou with thy case, the habit,
> Wrench awe from fools . . .
> > Angelo, *Measure for Measure*, act II, scene iv

LAO TZU:

> Pleasant sounds attract superficial listeners,
> Tao seems too simple to be interesting.

SHAKESPEARE:

So may the outward shows be least themselves—
The world is still deceiv'd by ornament.

Bassanio, *The Merchant of Venice*,
act III, scene ii

―――――

COMMENT: If names and outward appearances don't actually have much reality, then maybe whatever exists beyond any superficial artifice *is* real. Knowing that is probably a great secret, and valuable knowledge. Having that kind of knowledge could be quite powerful.

Thirty-six

Lao Tzu:

> Being gentle
> will always overcome
> any hard obstacle,
> any strength.

Shakespeare:

> You bear a gentle mind, and heavenly blessings
> Follow such creatures.
>> Chamberlain, *Henry VIII*, act II, scene iv

> Since men prove beasts, let beasts bear gentle
>   minds.
>> *The Rape of Lucrece*, line 1148

> He hath borne himself beyond the promise of his
>   age, doing
> in the figure of a lamb the feats of a lion.
>   He hath
> indeed better bett'red expectation.
>> Messenger, *Much Ado About Nothing*,
>> act I, scene i

COMMENT: For most of human history, certain thinkers and leaders have tried to encourage human beings to be gentle with each other, from the Buddha and Jesus and saints from all cultures to great historical figures who've changed nations, even including modern icons like Gandhi or Martin Luther King or Mother Teresa—all have counseled some version of the idea that a soft answer can turn away wrath. It seems to be a difficult lesson for most people to learn.

Thirty-seven

LAO TZU:

Tao is always still and at rest,
and yet it does everything.
The unmoved mover
calls the All.

SHAKESPEARE:

'Tis with my mind
As with the tide swelled up unto his height
That makes a still stand, running neither way.
Northumberland, Henry IV, Part 2,
act II, scene iii

It were better to be eaten to death with a rust
Than to be scour'd to nothing with perpetual
   motion.
Lord Chief Justice, Henry VI, Part 2,
act I, scene ii

Alas, now pray you
Work not so hard. I would the lightning had
Burnt up those logs that you are enjoin'd to pile!
Miranda, The Tempest, act III, scene i

COMMENT: Passivity and inactivity are, in fact, actions. For example, certain kinds of ancient fighting techniques are based entirely on simply moving out of the way of the aggressor. Not only is there no contact at all, but the aggressor ends up looking ridiculous.

Thirty-eight

LAO TZU:

> When Tao is lost,
> "Pity" becomes the rule;
> when pity is lost,
> "Justice" becomes the rule.

———

COMMENT: According to the Zen master Joshu, "Nature is complete, and does not need the embellishment of social constructs or a nation's laws. If the Way cannot be followed, then rules and laws for governing rise up in its place."

———

SHAKESPEARE:

> Yet Nature is made better by no mean
> But Nature makes that mean; so over that art
> Which you say adds to Nature, is an art
> That Nature makes.
> > Polixenes, *The Winter's Tale*, act IV, scene iv

The rarer action is in virtue than in vengeance.
> Prospero, *The Tempest*, act V, scene i

Pity is the virtue of the law.
> Alcibiades, *Timon of Athens*, act III, scene v

Isabella: Yet show some pity.
Angelo: I show it most of all when I show justice.
> *Measure for Measure*, act II, scene ii

―――――

COMMENT: In general, the idea that any society would have to make up laws to keep people from doing the wrong thing already indicates the decay of that society. Every human being ought to have virtue, and should never need to be told what's right and what's wrong. But societies degenerate. And when they do, pity comes into being. And when pity degenerates, then justice takes over. This seems to make justice a sad assignation for any society, a tertiary stage of degeneration.

Thirty-nine

LAO TZU:

> The sky gained the All
> and was made clear,
> the earth took it in
> and was settled,
> the valleys received
> and were filled.
> All things,
> as they partook of nature,
> came alive.

SHAKESPEARE:

> Behold, the earth has roots,
> Within this mile break forth a hundred springs;
> The oaks bear mast, the briars scarlet heps;
> The bounteous huswife Nature on each bush
> Lays her fullness before you.
>   Timon, *Timon of Athens*, act IV, scene iii

> This our life, exempt from public haunt,
> Finds tongues in trees, books in running brooks,
> Sermons in stones, and good in everything
>   Duke Senior, *As You Like It*, act II, scene i

COMMENT: Nature is true, urban environs less so. More can be learned from listening to a waterfall or walking with bare feet in the sand than in any university classroom. But there may be more to verse thirty-nine of the Tao than a simple encouragement to adhere more to the natural world. The true nature of any human being or event or object is far more important than mere appearance. When someone recognizes the true nature of anything, everything comes alive.

Forty

LAO TZU:

> What-is came from what-is-not,
> and nothing always becomes something.

SHAKESPEARE:

> Nothing is but what is not.
> > Macbeth, *Macbeth*, act I, scene iii

> Nothing that is so is so.
> > Feste, *Twelfth Night*, act IV, scene ii

> This is all our world:
> We shall know nothing.
> > Arcite, *The Two Noble Kinsmen*,
> > act II, scene ii

COMMENT: Aside from a current understanding of physics, which seems to support the notion that there is no such thing as *nothing* (partly because it always becomes something), verse forty of the Tao seems to invite an examination of the word *nothing* as no-thing. If it's not a *thing*, what is it? Also, all of these quotes imply a contradictory establishment of opposites, that a thought necessarily creates its opposite, unless you can know nothing, in which case everything is a miracle.

Forty-one

LAO TZU:

> When genuine people hear the secret Tao,
> they strive to read it like a book.

SHAKESPEARE:

> In nature's infinite book of secrecy
> A little I can read.
>> Soothsayer, *Antony and Cleopatra*,
>> act I, scene ii

LAO TZU:

> When unformed people hear,
> they only laugh at it.

SHAKESPEARE:

> For what we lack we laugh.
>> Theseus, *The Two Noble Kinsmen*,
>> act V, scene iv

LAO TZU:

> This is because Tao seems wrong, too simple,
> boring.

The Truth seems misleading.
This is because the power of Tao is inverted,
hidden like a valley.

SHAKESPEARE:

'Tis so strange that,
Though the truth of it stands off as gross
As black and white, my eye will scarcely see it.

Henry, *Henry V*, act II, scene ii

COMMENT: The medieval Franciscan logician William
of Ockham is generally quoted as saying that "enti-
ties should not be multiplied unnecessarily," which is
often interpreted to mean that the simplest answer is
the best. (This is sometimes called Ockham's Razor.)
Still, many people needlessly complicate things, and
can't seem believe that the truth can be so simple.
It's easy to make fun of a simple truth. It's harder to
follow it.

Forty-two

Lao Tzu:

> Out of Tao comes the One,
> out of one come two,
> out of two: three.
> From three all things come.

Shakespeare:

> Why railest thou on thy birth? the heaven and
>   earth?
> Since birth, and heaven, and earth, all three do
>   meet
> In thee at once.
> Friar Laurence, *Romeo and Juliet*,
act III, scene iii

> Berowne: White-handed mistress, one sweet
>   word with thee.
> Princess: Honey, and milk, and sugar—there is
>   three.
> *Love's Labor's Lost*, act V, scene ii

———

Comment: The number three seems to be significant in most world philosophies and religions. Joseph

Campbell explains a Hindu origin myth this way: after an eternity, the All wanted to know itself, so it split in two; those two became parents of a third, and from that third all things came into existence. Most religious mythologies have a father, mother, and child trinity, though some refer to a father, a son, and a holy spirit. It's also worth noting that in all early human counting systems there was a 1-2-3 pattern, but it actually meant "one, two, many." In other words, early human beings had words for one and two, but after that, the number was unlimited.

Forty-three

LAO TZU:

A secret of the Tao that few know
is that softness is the only way
to truly overcome, no matter how hard the
resistance is.
A hard sword will break,
a gentle word will gain admittance.

SHAKESPEARE:

Your gentleness shall force,
More than your force move us to gentleness.
Duke Senior, *As You Like It*, act II, scene vii

Much rain wears the marble.
Richard, Duke of Gloucester, *Henry VI*,
act III, scene ii

No, good my lord, let's fight with gentle words,
Till time lend friends, and friends their helpful
swords.
Duke of Aumerle, *Richard II*, act III, scene iii

COMMENT: The Cambridge edition of the King James Bible says "A soft answer turneth away wrath" (Proverbs 15:1), but hidden beneath that concept lies a certain secret strength, especially noted in Richard's quote above: marble is hard, water is almost insubstantial, but enough rain can disintegrate the marble; enough water poured over rocky ground can create a Grand Canyon. That's the power of a soft answer.

Forty-four

LAO TZU:

> What is closer to your heart,
> your fame or your life?
> Are your possessions better than your life?
> Is it more painful losing your possessions,
> or gaining them?
> Fame and possessions are things you can lose,
> at great misery to your heart.
> Stop wasting time on them.

SHAKESPEARE:

> Glory grows guilty of detested crimes,
> When for fame's sake, for praise, an outward part,
> We bend to that the working of the heart.
> > Princess of France, *Love's Labor's Lost*,
> > act IV, scene i

> Honor for wealth, and of that wealth doth cost
> The death of all, and all together lost.
> > *The Rape of Lucrece*, line 146

COMMENT: Movie stars and philosophers alike agree. "Fame will go by and, so long, I've had you, fame. If it goes by, I've always known it was fickle. So at least it's something I experience, but that's not where I live" (Marilyn Monroe). "Wealth is like sea-water; the more we drink, the thirstier we become; and the same is true of fame" (Arthur Schopenhauer).

Forty-five

LAO TZU:

Whatever is most perfect seems imperfect.
Tao fills up everything, but seems empty.
The path of Tao is straight, but seems to most
eyes crooked.
The most skilled seem the most awkward.
The greatest speech seems almost incoherent.

SHAKESPEARE:

Love, therefore, and tongue-tied simplicity
In least speak most.
> Theseus, *A Midsummer Night's Dream*,
> act V, scene i

LAO TZU:

When you are cold, move.
When you are hot, stand still.
If it rains, cover yourself.

SHAKESPEARE:

When clouds are seen, wise men put on their
cloaks.
> Citizen, *Richard III*, act II, scene iii

COMMENT: Here's another admonition to simplicity, and to the notion that the simplest answer is the best. Still, a surprising number of human beings stand in the rain and complain that they're getting wet. The simplest answer to that is to come in out of the rain.

Forty-six

Lao Tzu:

> Where the Way rules,
> plow horses fertilize the fields;
> where the Way does not rule,
> war horses parade in the park.

Shakespeare:

> Richard: A horse! A horse! My kingdom for a
> horse!
>> *[Richard is slain by Richmond.]*

. . . .

> Richmond: Let them not live to taste this land's
> increase that would with treason wound this
> fair land's peace!
> Now civil wounds are stopped, and Peace lives
> again.
>> *Richard III*, act V, scene v

Lao Tzu:

> No sin can exceed incitement to envy.

When envy breeds unkind division,
There comes the ruin, there begins confusion.

Duke of Exeter, *Henry VI, Part 1*, act IV, scene i

Forty-seven

Lao Tzu:

> You can know the whole world
> without leaving your own home.
> As you go further,
> you know less,
> until every place is your native home.

Shakespeare:

> I could be bounded in a nutshell
> and count myself a king of infinite space.
> > Hamlet, *Hamlet*, act II, scene ii

> For where thou art, there is the world itself,
> With every several pleasure in the world.
> > Earl of Suffolk, *Henry VI, Part 2*,
> > act III, scene ii

> You had much ado to make his anchor hold,
> When you cast out, it still came home.
> > Camillo, *The Winter's Tale*,
> > act I, scene ii

When I was at home, I was in a better place,
but travelers must be content.

> Touchstone, *As You Like It*,
> act II, scene iv

COMMENT: It's possible to see the world in a grain of sand. It's preferable to see the world in someone else's eyes. Characters from Ulysses to Dorothy have learned the often hard-won lesson: East, West, Home is Best. Especially when every place is your home.

Forty-eight

LAO TZU:

> The scholar needs to know more every day,
> but Tao is learned by knowing less,
> and acquires knowledge
> by letting nature take its course.

SHAKESPEARE:

> To be well-favored is the gift of fortune,
> but to write and read comes by nature.
> > Dogberry, *Much Ado About Nothing*,
> > act III, scene iii

LAO TZU:

> Try not to think too much,
> thinking gets in the way of moving.

SHAKESPEARE:

> The native hue of resolution
> Is sicklied o'er with the pale cast of thought.
> > Hamlet, *Hamlet*, act III, scene i

LAO TZU:

> The Way is gained by daily loss, by unlearning.
> By letting go of thought, everything gets done.
> The world is won by those who let it go.

SHAKESPEARE:

> If I do grow great, I'll grow less.
>   Falstaff, *Henry IV, Part 1*, act V, scene iv

COMMENT: "The only thing that interferes with my learning is my education" (Albert Einstein). "Ignorance is not so terrible; too much cleverness and too much learning, are far more fatal" (Plato). "Instead of giving money to found colleges to promote learning, why don't they pass a constitutional amendment prohibiting anybody from learning anything? If it works as good as Prohibition did, why, in five years we would have the smartest race of people on earth" (Will Rogers).

Forty-nine

LAO TZU:

Great minds are selfless.
Their generosity is nature's
The needs of others are their only needs,
and to them he gives alike.

SHAKESPEARE:

That churchman bears a bounteous mind indeed,
A hand as fruitful as the land that feeds us
His dews fall everywhere.

Sir Thomas Lovell, *Henry VIII*,
act I, scene iii

LAO TZU:

Look with kindness on both the good and the
evil.
This is the virtue of Te.

SHAKESPEARE:

The sun with one eye vieweth all the world.

Lord Talbot, *Henry IV, Part 1*,
act I, scene ii

LAO TZU:

> With Tao nature, look on everyone
> as your own family.

SHAKESPEARE:

> One touch of nature makes the whole world kin.
> Ulysses, *Troilus and Cressida*,
> act III, scene iii

———

COMMENT: The word *Te* itself means virtue, but it's also the power through which Tao is actualized. The virtue of that power is to see everything, especially all opposites like good and evil, right and wrong, masculine and feminine, as the same, or at least part of the same continuum. This way of looking at the world imparts kindness to every observation, encourages generosity, and, indeed, makes the whole world kin.

Fifty

LAO TZU:

> If the spirit is filled,
> then the body will live,
> and death will find no entrance.

SHAKESPEARE:

> You are full of heavenly stuff, and bear the
>   inventory
> Of your best graces in your mind; the which
> You were not running o'er.
> Henry, *Henry VIII*, act III, scene ii

———

COMMENT: In a religious context, if you believe that your soul is your true self, and that soul is purified, then death has no meaning. Another take on this concept might come from physics: nothing is ever created or destroyed, it just changes form.

———

LAO TZU:

> So for the wise there is no danger,
> and for the good there is no fear.

SHAKESPEARE:

> Virtue is bold, and goodness never fearful.
> Vincentio, *Measure for Measure*,
act III, scene i

———

COMMENT: It is essential to overcome fear. "The enemy is fear. We think it is hate; but, it is fear" (Gandhi). Just about everyone seems to agree with Shakespeare and Lao Tzu, in one way or another, about how that's done. "People living deeply have no fear of death" (Anais Nin). "Who sees all beings in his own self, and his own self in all beings, loses all fear" (Isa Upanishad).

Fifty-one

LAO TZU:

> The power of Tao begins everything;
> the virtue of Te governs it.
> Perception makes form,
> Action brings form to fruition.
> But Tao does not possess;
> Te does not command,
> and so all natural perceptions and actions agree,
> harmonize with Tao of their own accord.

SHAKESPEARE:

> For government doth keep in one consent,
> Congreeing in a full and natural close, like music.
> Duke of Exeter, *Henry V*, act I, scene ii

COMMENT: Verse fifty-one is clearly another political statement, at least in part, encouraging rulers not to feel a sense of possession, and not to command in order to rule. Instead, Tao encourages harmony: the process of statehood should be primarily harmonious.

LAO TZU:

This is why it is better to let Tao lead
than to try to trudge along the path yourself.

SHAKESPEARE:

You should be ruled and led
By some discretion that discerns your state
Better than you yourself.

Regan, *King Lear*, act II, scene iv

———

COMMENT: The way to bring harmony into your your
life is to get Ego out of the way, out of the picture alto-
gether if you can manage it, and let something greater
take the lead.

Fifty-two

LAO TZU:

Life begins within the mother,
as the Universe is the mother of all things.
Understanding the mother makes it easier to
understand the children,
watching the children we can know the mother
better.
In this way, find the virtue of Te.

SHAKESPEARE:

The tree may be known by the fruit, as the fruit
   by the tree,
then peremptorily I speak it, there is virtue.
                    Falstaff, *Henry IV, Part 1*, act II, scene iv

LAO TZU:

Close your ears, stop letting things enter you,
and your life can be calm.
Be open to every influence,
and your life can be chaos.

SHAKESPEARE:

You cram these words into mine ears against
The stomach of my sense.

Alonso, *The Tempest*, act II, scene i

LAO TZU:

Knowing this, the vision is cleared,
Weaknesses are strengths,
And your own light illuminates everything.
This is Tao.

SHAKESPEARE:

When the gracious light
Lifts up his burning head, each under eye
Doth homage to his new-appearing sight,
Serving with looks his sacred majesty.

Sonnet 7, lines 1–4

———

COMMENT: Verse fifty-two of the *Tao* is sometimes interpreted, in part, as an approach to parenting and teaching. First, it's sometimes easier to understand a child when you understand her parents. Second, it's easier to teach a child specifics first, rather than everything in general. Third, leading children with clear thoughts helps them to see everything more clearly. In his context, of course, the concept of "mother," "teacher," and "child" are metaphorical.

Fifty-three

LAO TZU:

Tao is a wide path, and easy to follow.
Walk that path and calm your mind.
Still, people seem to prefer smaller paths:
The rulers seem dignified in fine clothes
while farms are wasted with weeds.
The rich gorge themselves on excess
while others go hungry.
This is not the way of nature.
This is not Tao.

SHAKESPEARE:

A turn or two I'll walk
To still my beating mind.
Prospero, The Tempest, act IV, scene i

To be possessed with double pomp
To guard a title that was rich before . . .
Is wasteful and ridiculous excess.
Salsbury, King John, act IV, scene ii

Nature falls into revolt when gold becomes her
object.
King Henry, Henry IV, Part 2, act IV, scene v

COMMENT: Some people find it hard to avoid the notion of Plato's cave when thinking about certain aspects of the Tao. Here we are, all of us, sitting in a darkened cave, backs to the doorway, watching shadows on the wall and thinking that they're real, when, in fact, the easiest thing in the world would be to turn around, stand up, and walk out into the actual world. It's that easy, but most people don't do it.

Fifty-four

LAO TZU:

> Set firmly in Tao, you cannot be uprooted,
> and your spirit will be fortified.

SHAKESPEARE:

> I am able now, methinks
> (Out of a fortitude of soul I feel),
> To endure more miseries and greater far
> Than my weak-hearted enemies dare offer.
> > Cardinal Wolsey, *Henry VIII*,
> > act III, scene ii

LAO TZU:

> Cultivate Tao in yourself and your own virtue
> will be genuine
> and overflow to your family.
> From your family, it may spill into the town.
> From your town, it fills your country.
> And from your country, it can be everywhere.

SHAKESPEARE:

How far that little candle throws his beams!
So shines a good deed in a naughty world.

Portia, *Merchant of Venice*,
act V, scene i

COMMENT: To make the world a better place, all you have to do, at first, is to take these ideas (as discussed by Lao Tzu and by Shakespeare and by countless other people) into your heart, and let them make you a better person. Once that happens, you can easily become a beacon that could, eventually, throw light everywhere.

Fifty-five

LAO TZU:

> Allowing the Tao to come in you
> makes you like an innocent child
> whom poisonous insects will not bite
> wild animals attack
> nor any weapon harm.

SHAKESPEARE:

> Come on, poor babe.
> Some powerful spirit instruct the kites and ravens
> To be thy nurse!
>> Antigonus, *The Winter's Tale*, act II, scene ii

> Innocence shall make false accusation blush,
> and tyranny tremble at patience.
>> Hermione, *The Winter's Tale*, act III, scene ii

> The trust I have is in mine innocence,
> And therefore I am bold and resolute.
>> Pandulph, *King John*, act III, scene iv

COMMENT: "Four-Year-Old Pari Yadav Falls from Tenth Floor of Mumbai High-rise, Miraculously Unharmed" (news headline, July 2. 2012).

In an early moment of Francois Truffaut's fact-based film *Small Change* (1976), a baby reaches for a cat on a windowsill of an upper floor of an apartment building and tumbles several stories to the ground, gets up entirely unhurt, and wonders where the cat is. Someone else says, "If that had been an adult, she'd be dead." An earlier Truffaut film, *The Wild Child* (1970), recounts the true story of a boy discovered in rural France in the eighteenth century who had, apparently, been living in the woods alone all his life, almost certainly abandoned as an infant. Impossibly, he survived for eleven years on his own. Nature often seems to conspire to protect the innocent.

Fifty-six

LAO TZU:

Those who know don't talk,
those who talk don't know.
Better to listen.

SHAKESPEARE:

Speak less than thou knowest.
> Fool, *King Lear*, act I, scene iv

Give thy thoughts no tongue . . .
give every man thy ear
but few thy voice.
> Polonius, *Hamlet*, act I, scene iii

Talkers are no good doers.
> Murderer, *Richard III*, act I, scene iii

I think the best grace of wit will shortly run into
    silence,
and discourse grow commendable in none but
    only parrots.
> Lorenzo, *The Merchant of Venice*,
> act III, scene v

COMMENT: This is the greatest paradox in the world of sharing knowledge: anyone who knows the genuine truth of the universe doesn't talk about it; anyone who talks about it doesn't really understand it at all. Or as Jean-Jacques Rousseau puts it, "People who know little are usually great talkers, while men who know much say little." Which has to mean, unfortunately, that Lao Tzu and Shakespeare, along with the author of this book, don't really know what they're talking about.

Fifty-seven

LAO TZU:

You can gain ease by refraining.

SHAKESPEARE:

Refrain tonight,
And that shall lend a kind of easiness.
                              Hamlet, *Hamlet*, act III, scene iv

LAO TZU:

If laws increase only to frighten,
there is more crime.

SHAKESPEARE:

We must not make a scarecrow of the law
Setting it up to fear the birds of prey.
                              Angelo, *Measure for Measure*, act II, scene i

LAO TZU:

When weapons increase to deter conflict,
there is more war.
This is a way to chaos.
So refrain from laws and weapons.

SHAKESPEARE:

Make war breed peace.

> Alcibiades, *Timon of Athens*, act V, scene iv

———

COMMENT: Verse fifty-seven is another admonition first to rulers, but also to anyone who hopes to rule himself or herself. First, let go of the concept that you're in charge. Second, if you make up rules just to scare people, the rules are going to be doomed to failure. So let go of rules. Finally, let go of conflict, especially great conflicts that involve weapons, either guns or words. Let something better in yourself take the lead, something that doesn't need rules or weapons.

Fifty-eight

LAO TZU:

> When government is generous, and everyone
> has a say, everyone is happy.
> When government is cruel, people are rebellious.

SHAKESPEARE:

> The eagle suffers little birds to sing.
>> Tamora, *Titus Andronicus*, act IV, scene iv

———

COMMENT: This has often been interpreted as an admonition to democracy, but it's also clearly just an encouragement to fairness.

———

LAO TZU:

> There's a saying: "Bad luck brings good luck,
> good luck brings bad luck."

SHAKESPEARE:

'Tis a lucky day, boy, and we'll do good deeds
   on't.

> Shepherd, *The Winter's Tale*, act III, scene iii

COMMENT: Here Shakespeare and Lao Tzu seem to disagree. Is Lao Tzu saying that opposites attract? Shakespeare had, at least in his art, a superstitious mind, and good luck, while fickle, was always a good thing.

LAO TZU:

But that's nonsense, these things don't happen
   magically.
Good is a result of good, bad a result of bad.

SHAKESPEARE:

Good alone is good.

> King of France, *All's Well That End's Well*,
> act II, scene iii

COMMENT: Ah, wait—they do agree.

LAO TZU:

So if you're smart, you'll relax a little.
Be honorable, be generous, and everyone will
be yours.

SHAKESPEARE:

Your honor has through Ephesus pour'd forth
Your charity, and hundreds call themselves
Your creatures.

Gentleman, *Pericles*, act III, scene ii

Fifty-nine

LAO TZU:

> There is a saying: "To lead people or to serve God,
> there is nothing that provides security like abundance."

SHAKESPEARE:

> Well, he may sleep in security,
> for he hath the horn of abundance.
> > Falstaff, *Henry IV, Part 2*, act I, scene ii

———

COMMENT: Nothing makes a greater revolution than the lack of bread.

———

LAO TZU:

> This only means that saving up stores beforehand increases the well-being of everyone in times of need.

But it also means spiritual abundance,
and for that, there is Tao, which is an infinite
resource of power,
fills you with the virtues that allow you to lead
people and serve God.

SHAKESPEARE:

The king-becoming graces,
As justice, verity, temp'rance, stableness,
Bounty, perseverance, mercy, lowliness
Devotion, patience, courage, fortitude.
                    Malcolm, *Macbeth*, act IV, scene iii

Sixty

LAO TZU:

> Rule a large country
> as you would cook a small fish,
> simply and carefully.

SHAKESPEARE:

> While others fish with craft for great opinion,
> I with great truth catch mere simplicity.
> Whilst some with cunning gild their copper
>   crowns,
> With truth and plainness I do wear mine bare.
> > Troilus, *Troilus and Cressida*, act IV, scene iv

LAO TZU:

> In the perfect land, there is no ruler.
> There is no duty or work,
> there are no rich or poor,
> and all are innocent.

SHAKESPEARE:

> I' th' commonwealth I would, by contraries,
> Execute all things; for no kind of traffic
> Would I admit; no name of magistrate;

Letters should not be known; riches, poverty,
And use of service none; contract, succession,
Bourn, bound of land, tilth, vineyard, none;
No use of metal, corn, or wine, or oil,
No occupation, all men idle, all;
And women too, but innocent and pure;
No sovereignty.

Gonzalo, *The Tempest*, act II, scene i

COMMENT: Thomas Paine's *Common Sense* believed that "government, even in its best state, is but a necessary evil; in its worst state, an intolerable one." Quotes attributed to Thomas Jefferson amplify: "My reading of history convinces me that most bad government results from too much government. That government is best which governs the least, because its people discipline themselves." If people would discipline themselves, there would be no need for government.

Sixty-one

LAO TZU:

> A great person should be like a river
> that empties itself into all people.
> A great person should want nothing more
> Than to unite and feed the people.
> Greatness lies in service,
> and in that service lies great strength.

SHAKESPEARE:

> His state empties itself as doth an inland brook
>   into the main waters.
> > Portia, *Merchant of Venice*, act V, scene i

> So service shall with steeled sinews toil.
> And labor shall refresh itself with hope
> To do your Grace incessant services.
> > Lord Scroop, *Henry V*, act II, scene ii

———

COMMENT: T. E. Lawrence said of the great Bedouin leader Auda ibu Tayi, "His hospitality was sweeping; his generosity kept him always poor, despite the profits of a hundred raids." A great leader ought to be judged by how much he gives away.

Sixty-two

LAO TZU:

> The Tao is hidden deeply in all things, like a
> treasure.
> Let the wealthy grow in riches,
> and they will suffer
> while you mine in Tao
> for knowledge of yourself.
> That is the greatest jewel of all.

SHAKESPEARE:

> Who would not wish to be from wealth exempt,
> Since riches point to misery and contempt?
> > Flavius, *Timon of Athens*, act IV, scene ii

> I know myself now, and I feel within me
> A peace above all earthly dignities.
> > Wolsey, *Henry VIII*, act III, scene ii

COMMENT: The only real purpose in life is to find out
who and what you really are, and then to try as hard
as you can to be that. That's your real job. Everything
else is ridiculous.

Sixty-three

LAO TZU:

Nature acts in repose, works passively.

SHAKESPEARE:

Our foster-nurse of nature is repose.
> Doctor, *King Lear*, act IV, scene iv

LAO TZU:

The wise relish all things and requite anger with
virtue.

SHAKESPEARE:

To be in anger is impiety.
> Alcibiades, *Timon of Athens*, act III, scene v

Rage must be withstood.
> Richard, *Richard II*, act I, scene i

LAO TZU:

The wise perform great acts
but are contented to be unknown to all
because they act within,
and so rule the all.

SHAKESPEARE:

My crown is in my heart, not on my head . . .
Not to be seen. My crown is called content.
Henry, *Henry VI, Part 3*, act III, scene iii

COMMENT: Is requiting anger with virtue the same as turning the other cheek? Is working passively the same as passive resistance? These are difficult lessons to follow, except occasionally when you can be at rest, be content, and look inside. On those rare occasions, these lessons seem obvious and plain. If we could only hold on to that inner recognition. Unfortunately, it usually slips away.

Sixty-four

LAO TZU:

Take care of things before they are a problem.
It is easier to move small stones one by one
than to try to pick up a mountain.
It is easier to plant a seed
than to transplant a tree.
And, as is so often said:
the journey of a thousand miles
begins with the first step.
This way you have nothing to fear.

SHAKESPEARE:

Things done well and with a care exempt themselves from fear.

King Henry, *Henry VII*, act I, scene ii

COMMENT: Of course it would be great to take care of every difficulty before it got to be a really big problem. When that's not possible, it's comforting to remember that anything can be accomplished in small increments, in bite-sized pieces. In the autumn of 1705, Bach decided that he had to hear the great organist

Dietrich Buxtehude play, even though the concert was in a town two hundred miles away. Bach set out walking to the concert. He traveled as much as he could each day, and then slept by the side of the road, or in barns or farmhouses. It took weeks, but he eventually met his idol, learned from him, and walked home, where he then began to compose in earnest.

Sixty-five

LAO TZU:

> Preserve the simplicity of life.
> Better to eat according to the size of your belly,
> dress to fit your body,
> that way there is no poverty or envy
> and all are generous and content.
> This returns us to primal peace.

SHAKESPEARE:

> I earn that I eat, get that I wear,
> owe no man hate, envy no man's happiness,
> glad of other men's good, content with my harm,
> and the greatest of my pride is to see my ewes
>   graze.
>
> > Corin, *As You Like It*, act III scene ii

> Beauty, Truth, and Rarity,
> Grace in all simplicity.
>
> > *The Phoenix and Turtle*, lines 53–54

COMMENT: It's a gift to be simple, and a great secret to happiness. When you're hungry, eat. When you're tired, sleep. When you work, don't be distracted, just do the work. Unfortunately, even if this kind of simplicity can, occasionally, be accomplished, most people have to be reminded about it over and over again.

Sixty-six

LAO TZU:

> A river is the lowest thing in a valley,
> but remember that the river made the valley.
> That's the way to help people: as nature does.
> You should be led by the river.

SHAKESPEARE:

> The gentleman is learn'd, and a most rare
>   speaker,
> To nature none more bound; his training such
> That he may furnish and instruct great teachers.
> King Henry, Henry VIII, act I, scene ii

> Nature must obey necessity.
> Brutus, Julius Caesar, act IV, scene iii

> Nature's bequest gives nothing, but doth lend,
> And being frank she lends to those are free.
> Sonnet 4, lines 3–4

LAO TZU:

Learn from nature and you may teach teachers.

SHAKESPEARE:

The gentleman is learned.
To nature none more bound; his training such
That he may furnish and instruct great teachers.
King Henry, *Henry VIII*, act I, scene ii

COMMENT: Speaking in *Emile*, a major treatise on natural education, Rousseau says, "Nature will never deceive us." When he turned his concepts on himself, he came to a clear realization. "I have resolved on an enterprise that has no precedent and will have no imitator. I want to set before my fellow human beings a man in every way true to nature; and that man will be myself."

Sixty-seven

LAO TZU:

> Most of the world will say
> that Tao is foolish.
> This is because it's so genuine,
> but does not proclaim itself,
> and much of the world
> is not a genuine place.

SHAKESPEARE:

> Wisdom cries out in the streets, and no man
>   regards it.
>> Prince, *Henry IV, Part 1*, act I, scene ii

> Truth hath a quiet breast.
>> Bullingbrook, *Richard II*, act I, scene iii

> Truth hath better deeds than words to grace it.
>> Proteus, *The Two Gentlemen of Verona*,
>> act II, scene iii

———

COMMENT: Fellow Nazarenes laughed at Jesus when he tried to tell them what he thought was the truth.

The Dalai Lama has spent a lifetime trying to get the Chinese government to listen to him about the simplest truths, and they've ignored him. But the good news comes from Gandhi: "First they ignore you, then they laugh at you, then they fight you, then you win."

Sixty-eight

LAO TZU:

> The best soldier is not violent
> or filled with hate.

SHAKESPEARE:

> May that soldier a recreant [coward] prove
> That means not, hath not, or is not in love.
> > Agamemnon, *Troilus and Cressida*,
> > act I, scene iii

LAO TZU:

> A great commander
> becomes one with the multitude
> and is humble.

SHAKESPEARE:

> Is not the king's name twenty-thousand names?
> > Richard, *Richard II*, act III, scene ii

LAO TZU:

> To keep peace and harmony
> is to rise in heavenly virtue.

SHAKESPEARE:

> The fingers of the powers above do tune
> The harmony of this peace.
>> Philharmonus, *Cymbeline*, act V, scene v

> Blessed are the peacemakers on earth.
>> Henry, *Henry VI, Part 2*, act II, scene i

COMMENT: Verse sixty-eight is most often interpreted not as a paean to pacifism, but an admonition toward peace. Sometimes you have to fight, but if you do, try not to do it out of hatred. And you should try to remember that the person you're fighting is, in some great measure, you. Knowing that can only lead to peace, or at least the cessation of fighting.

Sixty-nine

LAO TZU:

> Ancient battle strategists had a saying:
> "To retreat a foot is better than advancing an
> inch."
> Don't march in formation, or appear too
> prepared;
> don't charge in frontal attack, or arm yourself
> with elaborate weapons.
> Hide your true face.
> Most of all, don't underestimate your enemy.
> What is the way?
> The passive, recessive one
> will always be the victor.

SHAKESPEARE:

> My face I'll grime with filth,
> Blanket my loins, elf all my hairs in knots,
> And with presented nakedness outface
> The winds and persecutions of the sky.
> > Edgar, *King Lear*, act II, scene iii

> The better part of valor is discretion.
> > Falstaff, *Henry IV, Part 1*, act V, scene iv

COMMENT: Verse sixty-nine of the *Tao* is generally thought to be its most direct advice on warfare. First consider Bernard of Clairvaux's thought, "Trees and stones will teach you what you cannot learn from masters." Then think of Francis Marion in the American Revolutionary War (known as The Swamp Fox), possibly the inventor of guerrilla war. He consistently prevailed against perpetually superior forces by using the natural elements, by making the swamps near Charleston his allies. Finally regard Sun Tzu's advice: "Be extremely subtle, even to the point of formlessness. Be extremely mysterious, even to the point of soundlessness. Thereby you can be the director of the opponent's fate."

Seventy

LAO TZU:

> These teachings are easy
> to understand and to practice,
> because they are lessons of nature,
> but they cannot be grasped
> by glancing and superficial study,
> and so there are few that understand.

SHAKESPEARE:

> Study is like the heaven's glorious sun,
> That will not be deep-searched by saucy looks.
> > Berowne, *Love's Labor's Lost*, act I, scene i

> When a man's verses cannot be understood,
> nor a man's good wit seconded with . . .
> > understanding,
> it strikes a man more dead
> than a great reckoning in a little room.
> > Touchstone, *As You Like It*, act III, scene iii

Nature works . . . which doth give me
A more content in course of true delight
Than to be thirsty after tottering honor,
Or tie my pleasure up in silken bags,
To please the fool.

Cerimon, Pericles, act III, scene ii

———————

COMMENT: You can't understand everything about mathematics if you only learn to add. You can't paint great work if you only paint by number. You can't be a guitar virtuoso if you only know three chords. Still, it is, ultimately, easy to master the geometry of the universe, the beauty of great art, and the subtlety of music, because they are all naturally occurring in you. Anyone can do it. It just takes more time and concentration than most people are willing to give.

Seventy-one

LAO TZU:

> To know you do not know, that is best.
> Presuming you know is a disease.
> The wise have healthy minds.
> because they do not go contrary to nature.

SHAKESPEARE:

> Angelo: Either you are ignorant, or seem so,
>   craftily.
> Isabella: Let me be ignorant, but graciously to
>   know I am no better.
>> *Measure for Measure*, act II, scene iv

> His ignorance were wise,
> Where now his knowledge must prove ignorance.
>> Princess, *Love's Labor's Lost*, act II, scene i

COMMENT: "I am the wisest man alive, for I know one thing, and that is that I know nothing" (Plato in *The Republic*). "God is best known in not knowing him"

(Augustine of Hippo). It might be a prudent thing to question anyone who tells you that they know more than you do. Of course, sometimes they do, because you don't know everything.

Seventy-two

LAO TZU:

> Do not seek to love people.
> Modestly love yourself,
> and their love will come to you.

SHAKESPEARE:

> Love sought is good, but love unsought is better.
> Olivia, Twelfth Night, act III, scene i

LAO TZU:

> Know your secret self,
> and you will have your life.

SHAKESPEARE:

> What I am, and what I would, are as secret as
> maidenhead.
> Viola, Twelfth Night, act I, scene v

LAO TZU:

> The wise never reveal themselves.
> They say they are nothing.

The quality of nothing hath not such need to hide itself.

Gloucester, King Lear, act I, scene ii

COMMENT: If you can see yourself in everything, it's easier to love everything as you love yourself. There's also a story about a man who thought nothing of himself or anything around him because he was so much in love with his wife. He followed her around, loving everything she touched: a lamppost that she brushed up against, the button on the street corner that she pushed to change the light to green. His obsession grew to hilarious proportions before he realized that if he was to truly love her, he had to love all things, including himself.

Seventy-three

LAO TZU:

> Not by words
> does Tao speak to the heart.

SHAKESPEARE:

> But words are words; I never did hear
> That the bruised heart was pierced through
>   the ear.
>> Barbantio, *Othello*, act I, scene iii

LAO TZU:

> The wise do not call out
> and yet all things come to them.

SHAKESPEARE:

> I have neither wit, nor words, nor worth,
> Action, nor utterance, nor the power of speech
> To stir men's blood; I only speak right on.
>> Antony, *Julius Caesar*, act III, scene ii

LAO TZU:

> Great plans are like the net of the Universe
> moving not in haste, but slow to unfold.

SHAKESPEARE:

> To plainness honor's bound
> When Majesty stoops to folly. Reserve thy state,
> And in thy best consideration check this hideous
>   rashness.
>
> Kent, *King Lear*, act I, scene i

———

COMMENT: Everything in the universe unfolds as it will, not with words or the actions of even the wisest people. And it unfolds in its own time. All you really have to do is try not to worry, and to let that happen.

Seventy-four

LAO TZU:

> There can be no purity
> in a nation that murders.
> Murder is against nature.

SHAKESPEARE:

> Pure thoughts are dead and still
> While lust and murder wakes to stain and kill.
> > *The Rape of Lucrece*, lines 167–168

> Murder most foul, as in the best it is,
> But this most foul, strange, and unnatural.
> > Ghost of Hamlet's Father, *Hamlet*, act I, scene v

LAO TZU:

> Executioners do more damage
> to themselves than to those they kill.

SHAKESPEARE:

> Your hangman is a more penitent trade than your
> bawd:
> he doth oft'ner ask forgiveness.
> > Pompey, *Measure for Measure*, act IV, scene ii

Lao Tzu:

> When death is rare,
> all will want to live.

Shakespeare:

> 'Tis a vile thing to die, my gracious Lord,
> When men are unprepar'd and look not for it.
>> Catesby, *Richard III*, act III, scene ii

———

Comment: For at least five thousand years, cultures have enforced laws against murder under any circumstance. So it's difficult to understand why human beings still kill each other, and with such eagerness. Is it that we don't agree with the law? How is it that we still can't manage to follow this advice?

Seventy-five

LAO TZU:

> All are unhappy
> when the ruler does not govern
> by the assent of the people.

SHAKESPEARE:

> He is a happy king, since he gains from his
>   subjects
> the name of good by his government.
>
> Pericles, Pericles, act II, scene i

LAO TZU:

> The best rule is abstinence from ruling,
> like water flowing.

SHAKESPEARE:

> He doth with holy abstinence subdue
> That in himself which he spurs on his power
> To qualify in others.
>
> Vincentio, Duke of Vienna, Measure for
Measure, act IV, scene ii

COMMENT: Verse seventy-five is another political statement about the best way to rule a society, and the admonitions from Lao Tzu and Shakespeare seem to agree that the assent of the people is an essential ingredient in good government. But where Lao Tzu continues his thought that the best rule is the least rule, Shakespeare takes the more Western view—and, in fact, a more Elizabethan-world-order view—that a harmonic agreement among all concerned is best. (This is a concept best expressed a bit later in John Dryden's poem "A Song for St. Cecilia's Day," which opens, "From harmony, from heavenly harmony, this universal frame began, when nature underneath a heap of jarring atoms lay.")

Seventy-six

LAO TZU:

> The living are yielding and supple,
> the dead are stiff and unbending.
> The stiffest tree
> is the first to crack in the storm.
> The quiet heart endures the storm.

SHAKESPEARE:

> The splitting wind makes flexible the knees of
>   the knotted oaks.
> > Nestor, *Troilus and Cressida*, act I, scene iii

> To wisdom he's a fool that will not yield.
> > Lord, *Pericles*, act II, scene iv

> I do oppose my patience to his fury, and am arm'd
> To suffer, with a quietness of spirit,
> The very tyranny and rage of his.
> > Antonio, *The Merchant of Venice*,
> > act IV, scene i

COMMENT: It might be interesting to note that the creation of exercises that involve stretches and postures arose from this concept. Certain disciplines like yoga seem to be able to keep aging at bay. But the concept goes well beyond the physical. The more flexible you are, the longer you'll live. The less agitated you get, the longer you'll live. The more you're at peace, the longer you'll live.

Seventy-seven

LAO TZU:

> Tao is like a drawn bow
> where the low is high and the high is low,
> because the string of humility makes it so.

SHAKESPEARE:

> I have sounded the base-string of humility.
> > Henry, *Henry IV, Part 1*, act IV, scene ii

> I swear, 'tis better to be lowly born
> And range with humble livers in content.
> > Anne, *Henry VIII*, act II, scene iii

> If it did infect my blood with joy
> Or swell my thought to any strain of pride,
> Let God for ever keep it from my head,
> And make me as the poorest vassal is
> That doth with awe and terror kneel to it.
> > Henry, *Henry IV, Part 1*, act IV, scene v

COMMENT: There's a story about a minister and his son driving on a crowded expressway. Another man in a

Cadillac is driving right behind them, almost on their bumper. The son says, "He's about to hit us." And the minister says, "It's all right. Be patient." Then the Cadillac veers around wildly and cuts in front of the minister's car. The son says, "He cut you off!" But the minister says, "It's all right. Be humble." They watch as the Cadillac continues to drive, nearly out of control, cutting in front of everyone, until it's out of sight. Five minutes later they come on the Cadillac pulled to the side of the expressway, getting a ticket from a very agitated patrolman. Every car the Cadillac passed is now sailing by. So the minister says to his son, "You can see that it's truly said, 'The first shall be last, and the mighty brought down.'"

Seventy-eight

LAO TZU:

> Nothing yields like water,
> but when it rushes like the seas,
> nothing can withstand it.
> This is the paradox
> of weakness prevailing
> over strength.

SHAKESPEARE:

> Be he the fire, I'll be the yielding water.
> > Bullingbrook, *Richard II*, act III, scene iii

> Let us be backed with God, and with the seas,
> Which hath he hath giv'n for fence impregnable.
> > Lord Hastings, *Henry VI, Part 3*,
> > act IV, scene i

> I am not made of stone,
> But penetrable to your kind entreaties.
> > Glouceseter, *Richard III*, act III, scene vii

COMMENT: There are a lot of verses in the *Tao* concerning or employing paradox. One thing is true but its opposite is also true. You win by surrender. You achieve by doing nothing. Everything empty is full. The virtue of paradox is that it's useful in breaking a linear train of thought. It can be something as painful and hilarious as Hegel's "We learn from history that we do not learn from history." It can be something as beautiful and mind-bending as the Borges *alph*, a point in space that contains all other points. The use of paradox in this context seems to be to help thinking break free from predictable patterns, and to suddenly see something new.

Seventy-nine

LAO TZU:

There is no value in dispute and quarreling.
The virtuous do not take sides
and promote agreement and harmony.

SHAKESPEARE:

Quarreling is valor misbegot,
and came into the world when
sects and factions were newly born.
> Senator, *Timon of Athens*, act III, scene v

LAO TZU:

It has been said that, though the Tao is impartial
it always favors the good. Another paradox.

SHAKESPEARE:

Thy head is as full of quarrels
as an egg is full of meat,
and yet thy head hath been beaten
as addle as an egg for quarreling.
> Mercutio, *Romeo and Juliet*, act III, scene i

If the great gods be just, they shall assist
The deeds of justest men.

        Pompey, *Antony and Cleopatra*, act II, scene i

———

COMMENT: Another paradox: don't take sides, but always be on the side of the good. Less paradoxical: don't argue incessantly, you'll never get anywhere.

Eighty

LAO TZU:

> The perfect land is small,
> with few people,
> unless those people think too much.

SHAKESPEARE:

> They say there's but five upon this isle:
> we are three of them, if th' other two
> be brain'd like us, the state totters.
>> Trinculo, *The Tempest*, act III, scene ii

LAO TZU:

> The perfect land is harmonious.

SHAKESPEARE:

> The man that hath no music in himself,
> Is fit for treasons, stratagems, and spoils,
> Let no such man be trusted.
>> Lorenzo, *The Merchant of Venice*, act V, scene i

LAO TZU:

In the perfect land,
there is reverence
for what has come before.

SHAKESPEARE:

Sir, he made a chimney in my father's house,
and the bricks are alive at this day to testify it;
therefore deny it not.

Smith the Weaver, Henry VI, Part 2,
act IV, scene ii

COMMENT: Paradise, then, is small, harmonious, and built on a firm foundation of the past. It's that simple.

Eighty-one

LAO TZU:

The truth doesn't always sound great in words,
great-sounding words aren't always the truth.

SHAKESPEARE:

They that dally nicely with words may quickly
   make them wanton.
> Viola, *Twelfth Night*, act III, scene i

Moth: They have been at a great feast of words,
   and stol'n the scraps.
Custard: O, they have liv'd long on the alms-
   basket of words.
> *Love's Labor's Lost*, act V, scene i

LAO TZU:

The truly wise don't know many things,
anyone who knows many things isn't truly wise.

SHAKESPEARE:

This is a gift that I have, simple, simple.
> Holofernes, *Love's Labor's Lost*,
> act IV, scene ii

Let me be ignorant, and in nothing good,
But graciously to know I am no better.

> Isabella, *Measure for Measure*, act II, scene iv

Better a witty fool than a foolish wit.

> Feste, *Twelfth Night*, act I, scene v

Nothing that is so is so.

> Feste, *Twelfth Night*, act IV, scene i

———

COMMENT: *The Book of Tao* seems to conclude by reiterating that words are no good in communicating its ideas, and that everyone who writes about it doesn't really know what they're talking about. So why have a book like this at all? There was a teacher who was lecturing about various cloud formations, and the students weren't paying much attention. So she took the class outside, to show them what she was talking about. Every time she'd mention a new cloud, she'd find it in the sky, point it out, staring up at it and talking about it. After a minute she looked at the class and realized that they were all staring at her pointing finger. This book is a pointing finger. You should probably stop reading it now, and look up.

Conclusion

SHAKESPEARE:

A good play needs no epilogue.

Epilogue, *As You Like It*

LAO TZU:

Once you've made your point, don't brag.